Startling Hocus Pocus Trivia

Hocus Pocus Trivia That Will Make You Love The Movie Even More

DEDICATION

Contents

Introduction

Whenever Halloween rolls around, one of the Disney movies we always watch is Hocus Pocus. But just because you know it like the back of your hand, does not mean you're prepared for our super-hard trivia quiz. As a '90s kid, I grew up watching Hocus Pocus over and over again every Halloween. For years I wanted a black cat named Binx and I longed to go to Salem, Massachusetts and meet real, live witches. As an adult, I won't lie—15 Hocus Pocus Facts That Will Make You Love The Movie Even More I squealed with joy when I had the opportunity to visit Salem and see some of the locations where the movie was filmed.

To this day, Hocus Pocus remains a cult classic amongst fans of all ages.! In our humble opinion, it's one of the best movies to see when you're in the mood for something spooky (but not too spooky). Hocus Pocus tells the heartwarming tale of three elderly womens' eternal quest for youth at any cost, as well as a subplot of the chronic shame that comes with being a big old virgin.

It's a classic movie that came into our lives in a year that I cannot say here because that is the first quiz question and I am not here to spoon-feed your victory, as much as I would like to.

Are you ready for the sequel that is probably never going to come?

Let's find out, champ.Grab a broomstick (or vacuum) and fly through the questions below!

1

QUESTIONS

1. Let's start with an easy one: What's the first line of the movie?

    A.   Oh look, another glorious morning

    B.   Emily?

2. Who directed Hocus Pocus?

    A.   Mark Rosman
    B.   Kenny Ortega

3. What was a key ingredient in the witches' life potion?

    A.   dead man's toe
    B.   dead man's nose

4. What's Ice's real name?

A.   Ernie

B.   Joey

5. What was Max "dressed as" when he took Dani trick-or-treating ?

A. Tom Cruise
B. a rapper

6. What was the name of Winnie's old flame?

A.   Billy Butcherson
B.   Bobby Bones

7. Who played the devil?

A. Hector Elizondo
B. Garry Marshall

8. What did Max's parents dress as for Halloween?

    A.   Dadcula and Madonna
    B.   Frankenstein and Cher

9. What was the name of the high school that Max attends?

A.   Jacob Bailey High School
B.   Salem High School

10. And last but not least: When was the film released?

A.   October 1993
B.   July 1993

11. Who was driving the bus when Binx the cat gets run over?

A.   Winifred Sanderson
B.   Sarah Sanderson

12. What is Ice the bully's real name?

A.   Jay
B.   Ernie

13. When the Sanderson sisters are hung, we get a glimpse of Winifred's socks. What color are they?
    A.   Green
    B.   Red

14. After Max yells at Dani while trick-or-treating, how does he cheer her up?

    A.   Makes a funny face
    B.   Tickles her

15. Which is NOT an insult Billy calls Winifred when he's finally able to speak?

    A.   Witch
    B.   Wench

16. Jason Marsden, who voiced Binx the cat, also voiced which famous Disney character?

    A.   Max Goof from "A Goofy Movie"
    B.   Stitch from "Lilo & Stitch"

17. What are the last four digits of Max's phone number he gives Allison?

    A.   9142
    B.   1692

18. What was the name of Thackery's little sister?

    A.   Sarah

    B.   Emily

19. What was Max and Dani's dad dressed up as at the costume party?

    A.   Skeleton

    B.   Vampire

20. Which Disney character did Dani want Max to dress up as next Halloween?

    A.   Peter Pan

    B.   Pluto

21. Right before the Sanderson sisters kidnap the bullies, what had the guys been doing?

    A.   Teepeeing a house

B.   Egging a house

22. Who said, "It's a full moon tonight. That's when all the weirdos are out."

A.   Allison
B.   Dani

23. How many cats played Binx?

A.   Seven
B.   Nine

24. Why does Binx confront the witches at the beginning of the movie?
A. Curiosity made the cat immortal
B. Curiosity killed the cat
C. They kidnapped his sister
D. His friends dared him to
25. Which actor was Max's role originally offered to?
A. Colin Farrell
B. Robert Downey Jr
C. Brad Pitt
D. Leonardo Dicaprio
26. What are the witches called, according to legend?
A. THE SANDERSON TWINS
B. THE EVIL WITCHES OF SALEM
C. THE ANDERSON SISTERS
D. THE SANDERSON SISTERS
27. What does Max and Dani's dad dress up as for Halloween?
A. A KNIGHT IN SHINING ARMOR
B. KING ARTHUR
C. COUNT DRACULA

D. PRINCE CHARMING

28. What's the name of the zombie the witches bring back to life?
    A. BILLY BUTCHERSON
    B. BILLY SANDERSON
    C. ANDIE ANDERSON
    D. OMRI KATZ

29. How do the kids get away from the witches at first?
    A. THEY ALERT THE AUTHORITIES
    B. THEY SIC AN ANGRY MOB OF PARENTS ON THEM
    C. THEY LOCK THEM IN THE SCHOOL KILN
    D. THEY RUN THEM OVER WITH A BUS

30. What year did the movie first come out?

    A. 1993
    B. 2001
    C. 1996
    D. 1999

31. How long has it been since the witches were burned at the stake?

    A. 700 YEARS
    B. 500 YEARS
    C. 150 YEARS
    D. 300 YEARS

32. How do the witches lure their prey?

    A. THEY LURE THEM WITH A TRAIL OF CRUMBS
    B. THEY HYPNOTIZE THE CHILDREN WITH THEIR SINGING
    C. THEY KIDNAP THEM IN THEIR SLEEP

D. THEY USE THE BOOK TO CAST SPELLS ON THEM

33. What will happen to the witches at sunrise?

A. THEY WILL TURN TO DUST
B. THEY WILL GO HUNGRY AND DIE
C. ALL OF THE ABOVE
D. THE GHOSTS OF THEIR VICTIMS WILL HAUNT THEM FOREVER

34. What is this character's first name?

A. MARY
B. WINIFRED

C. EMILY

D. SARAH

35. How do the witches stay young forever?

A. THEY FEED ON THE SOULS OF YOUNG CHILDREN

B. THEY GAVE THEIR SOULS TO THE DEVIL

C. THEY'RE PRETTY MUCH INVINCIBLE

D. THEY SACRIFICE EACH OTHER, THEN COME BACK TO LIFE

36. What year is it when the Sanderson Sisters are hanged?

A. 1693

B. 1692

37. What's the name of the Thackery Binx's friend at the start of the film?

A. Elijah

B. William

38. What is the name of the potion that will keep the Sanderson Sisters alive forever?

A. Eternal Life Spell

B. Life Potion

39. Where did Max's family live before moving to Salem?

A. New York City

B. Los Angeles

40. What does Winifred tell the angry Salem townsfolk?

A. Don't get your knickers in a twist!

B. We're just spending a quiet evening at home!

41. What color is Max's bike?

A. Red
B. Lime Green

42. What type of people are out because of the full moon according to Dani?

A. Weirdos
B. Idiots

43. What does Max tell his dad that he's dressed as for Halloween?

A. A Rapper
B. A little leaguer

44. The bones of how many children are buried in the walls that surround the Sanderson house?

A. 100
B. 500

45. How many times were the words 'hocus pocus' used in the movie?

A. 3
B. 2

46. What is ICE's real name?

A. Ernie
B. Eddie

47. What is Winifred's spell book bound in?

A. Human skin
B. Fat of a hangman

48. What year (present day) do the Sanderson Sisters return from the dead?

A. 1990
B. 1993

49. What is the name of the talking black cat?

A. Max
B. Paws
C. Binx

50. Who says this quote: "So take her to the movies like a normal person"?

A. Dani
B. Max
C. Jay
D. Allison

51. What was Sarah's response after Winifred said, "Why? Why was I cursed with such idiot sisters?"

A. "We're not idiots!"

B. "Just lucky, I guess."

C. "Cat's got my tongue."

52. What actress plays Sarah Sanderson?

A. Vinessa Shaw

B. Kathy Najimy

C. Sarah Jessica Parker

53. Leonardo DiCaprio was offered the role of Max before Omri Katz was.

A. True

B. False

54. Thora Birch plays the role of Dani.

A. True
B. False

55. At the beginning of the film, the Sanderson sisters were executed for witchcraft.

A. True
B. False

56. What is the name of the Halloween-hating teenager ?

A. Max Dennison
B. Harry Potter
C. Kenny Ortega
D. Luke Skywalker

57.

Where does this story take place ?

  A. Los Angeles
  B. New York
  C. London
  D. Salem

58.

What are the names of the Sanderson sisters ?

  A. Lachesis, Clotho, Atropos
  B. Prue, Piper, Phoebe
  C. Winifred, Sarah, Mary
  D. Sarah, Bonnie, Nancy

59.

In what was Thackery Binx transformed ?

  A. a pumpkin
  B. a cat
  C. a candle
  D. a broom

60.

Where the Sanderson sisters hanged ?

  A. Yes
  B. No

61

What must be done in order to bring back the Sanderson sisters ?

A. a spell
B. a potion
C. a virgin has to lit a candle
D. a child has to be sacrificed

62.

Who does Max have a crush on ?

A. Emily
B. Allison
C. Mary
D. Julie

63.

What's the name of his little sister ?

A. Dani
B. Maryan
C. Sandy
D. Paula

64.

What happened when Allison, Dani and Max went to the Sanderson house ?

A. nothing
B. Max lit a candle and brought back the Sanderson sisters
C. Dani broke her leg
D. Allison and Max kissed

65.

Are the Sanderson sisters back for good ?

A. Yes

B. No

66

What must the sisters do in order to stay alive ?

A. suck the life out of all children in Salem

B. buy a new candle

C. kill Max

D. find a spellbook

67.

Can the cat talk ?

A. Yes

B. No

68.

What type of spell did the sisters cast on the grown-ups of Salem ?

A. sleeping spell

B. dancing spell

C. zombie spell

D. freezing spell

69.

How did the sisters find Max, Allison and Dani ?

A. with a location spell

B. the kids opened the sisters's spellbook, wich send a signal of its location

C. zombies found them

D. they didn't find them

70.

What must the sisters do in order to suck the life out of a child?

    A. the child must drink a potion
    B. the child must be eaten
    C. a spell
    D. a dance routine

71. Who drinks the potion at the end ?

    A. Allison
    B. Dani
    C. Binx
    D. Max

72. What happened to the sisters when the sun came up?

    A. they were transformed into statues and turned to dust
    B. they exploded
    C. they melted
    D. nothing

73. Which actress was Mary's role first offered to?

    A. MELISSA ANN MCCARTHY
    B. ROSIE O'DONNELL
    C. ROSEANNE BARR
    D. BETTE MIDLER

74. What is this character's first name?

A. BILLY
B. MAX
C. ZACHARY
D. THACKERY

75. Where did Max and Dani's family move from?

A. BOULDER, CO
B. AUSTIN, TX
C. LOS ANGELES, CA
D. SAN FRANCISCO, CA

76. True or False: Bette Midler has said that out of all her films, Hocus Pocus is her favorite.

A. TRUE
B. FALSE

77. What does Max and Dani's mom dress up as for Halloween?

A. A WITCH
B. A VAMPIRE

C. MADONNA

D. ANGELINA JOLIE

78. What song do the witches sing at the town's Halloween party?

A. WITCHCRAFT

B. I PUT A SPELL ON YOU

C. R-E-S-P-E-C-T

D. COME LITTLE CHILDREN

79. What is this character's first name?

A. EMILY

B. DANI

C. ALLISON

D. MARY

80. Who is the zombie, anyway?

A. WINIFRED'S DAD

B. SARAH'S EX-HUSBAND

C. WINIFRED'S BROTHER

D. WINIFRED'S UNFAITHFUL LOVER

81. Where does the movie take place?

A. YORKTOWN, VIRGINIA
B. ANDOVER, MASSACHUSETTS
C. SALEM, MASSACHUSETTS
D. CHARLESTON, SOUTH CAROLINA

82. How do the witches find the kids after they "die"?

A. AFTER THE KIDS OPEN THE BOOK, IT SUMMONS THEM
B. MAX'S LITTLE SISTER ACCIDENTALLY CASTS A SPELL
C. A VIRGIN (MAX) LIGHTS THE BLACK FLAME CANDLE
D. THE GHOSTS OF CHILDREN PAST SWARM THEIR HOUSE

83. What animal did the witches transform Binx into?

A. A UNICORN
B. A BLACK HORSE
C. A BLACK CAT
D. A BLACK DOG

84.

What did Thackery call Winifred which caused her to turn him into a cat?

    A. Evil
    B. Wretched
    C. Hag

85. Complete the Life Potion instructions: "One final thing and all is done, add a piece of thine own _____ "

    A. Saliva
    B. Tongue
    C. Hair

86. Why did Max end up taking Dani trick-or-treating?

A. Punishment for staying out late
B. Dani threatened to tell his crush about his feelings for her
C. Parents couldn't do it because they were going to a Halloween party

87. Max's bullies are called Jay and ___?

A. Thorn
B. Ice
C. Buck

88. What's so special about this candle?

A. Glow in the dark
B. Black flame
C. Never goes out

89. Who did Billy Butcherson cheat on Winifred with?

A. Sarah
B. Mary
C. Binx

90. What's the first thing Mary smells when she is revived?

A. Virgins
B. Trouble
C. Children

91. When Billy finally removes the stitches from his mouth, what's the first thing he calls Winifred?

A. Shrew
B. Devil
C. Wench

92. What is the only thing that can protect Max, Dani and Allison from the witches?

A. Lighting the black-flamed candle
B. A ring of salt
C. Having Winifred's book of spells in their possession

93. What is Mary's witching power?

    A. She can see in the dark
    B. She can move objects with her eyes
    C. She can smell children
    D. She can turn children into stone

94. Before Kathy Najimy was cast as Mary, which actress turned it down because she didn't want to play a witch who kills children?

A. Meg Ryan
B. Rosie O'Donnell
C. Julia Roberts
D. Julie Andrews

95. What is the story of the black-flamed candle?

A. If a virgin lights the candle on Halloween, the dead come back to life
B. If a non-virgin lights the candle on Halloween, spirits are banished forever

96. What was the talking cat's name?

A. Thackery Binx
B. Zachary Binx

97. Who does Dani want her and Max to go dressed as trick-or-treating the following year?

A. Wendy and Peter Pan

35

B. Winnie The Pooh and Piglet

C. The Sanderson sisters

D. Sonny and Cher

98. How do the Sanderson sisters end up dying at the end of the film?

A. They are tricked into walking into a furnace

B. Max, Dani and Allison throw salt at them

C. The sun rises

D. A virgin lights the black-flamed candle

99. At the beginning of the film Thackery Binx is transformed into a what?

A. Statue

B. Gravestone

C. Black cat

D. Lightning-struck tree

100. How long did it take the film to go from VHS to DVD?

  A. 4 years
  B. 2 years
  C. 8 years
  D. 12 year

101. After Thackery Binx is transformed, how many years pass before Max and his family move to Salem?

  A. 150
  B. 300
  C. 400

D. 105

102. Upon release, the film was considered:

   A. A critical success
   B. A commercial success
   C. A complete failure
   D. A cult classic

103. David Kirshner, the director, got the idea for the film when:

   A. A black cat walked by
   B. He broke a mirror
   C. He opened an umbrella inside
   D. He walked under a ladder

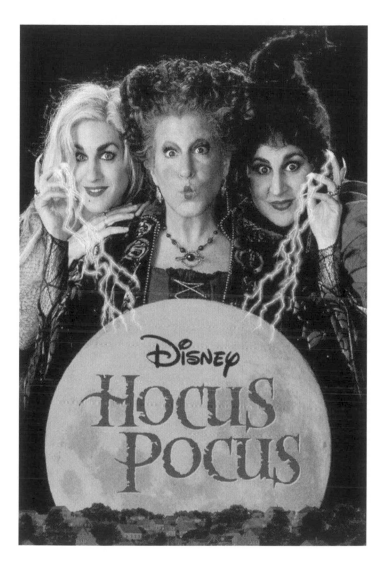

ANSWERS

1.   ANSWER: Emily

While Bette Midler's scorn for fall weather in this movie is *iconic*, the first scene actually shows Thackery Binx waking up to discover that Sanderson sisters lured his little sister Emily away.

2. ANSWER: Kenny Ortega

Ortega has also directed all three High School Musical movies and more than 10 episodes of Gilmore Girls.

3. ANSWER: dead man's toe

Other delicious-sounding additions include blood of owl and newt saliva. Yum.

4. ANSWER: Ernie

Anyone who goes so far as to shave "ICE" on the back of his head must really hate his given name.

5. ANSWER: A rapper

While Max tells his parents that his non-costume is "a rap singer," it's actually very versatile. Dani describes the getup as a "little leaguer" when the siblings encounter the town bullies.

6. **ANSWER: Billy Butcherson**

The actor behind the friendly zombie, Doug Jones, also starred as the amphibian man in *The Shape of Water* and the Silver Surfer in *Fantastic Four*. (In case you're wondering, Bobby Bones is a radio host currently on *Dancing With the Stars*.)

7. ANSWER: Garry Marshall

Yep, that's the *Pretty Woman* director dancing around in boxing shorts and red rubber gloves. Another fun fact: His real-life sister Penny Marshall played his wife — or Medusa, as Winnie initially suspects — in the film.

8.   ANSWER: Dadcula and Madonna

The Dennisons from the beginning of the film certainly didn't disappoint at the town hall party. Dani's face when she sees her mom in a cone bra is PRICELESS.

9.   ANSWER: Jacob Bailey High School

"Tis a prison for children!" Winnie says as she's lured into the quaint brick building. Unfortunately the actual elementary school that served as the filming location shut down not long after production (a.k.a. there's no kiln in there now).

10.   **ANSWER: July 1993**

Tricked ya! Even though it's a Halloween movie, *Hocus Pocus* came out in the dead of summer to not-so positive reviews. Luckily, people have come to realize this cult film's genius over time. You can catch it this year on Freeform during their 31 Days of Halloween celebration.

11.   Sarah Sanderson;
12.   Ernie;
13.   Green;
14.   Makes a funny face;
15.   Witch;
16.   Max Goof from *A Goofy Movie*;
17.   9142;

18.   Emily;
19.   Vampire;
20.   Peter Pan;
21.   Teepeeing a house;
22.   Dani;
23.   Nine
24.   THEY KIDNAPPED HIS SISTER
25.   LEONARDO DICAPRIO
26.   THE SANDERSON SISTERS
27.   COUNT DRACULA
28.   BILLY BUTCHERSON
29.   THEY LOCK THEM IN THE SCHOOL KILN
30.   1993
31.   300 YEARS
32.   THEY HYPNOTIZE THE CHILDREN WITH THEIR SINGING
33.   THEY WILL TURN TO DUST
34.   WINIFRED
35.   THEY FEED ON THE SOULS OF YOUNG CHILDREN

36.   A
37.   A
38.   B
39.   B
40.   A
41.   B
42.   A
43.   A
44.   A
45.   B
46.   A

47.   A
48.   B
49.   Binx.

Binx's full name is Thackery Binx. He was turned into a cat by the Sanderson sisters at the beginning of the film.

50.   Dani.

Dani says this to her brother Max.

51.   "Just lucky, I guess.".
52.   Sarah Jessica Parker.
53.   True
54.   True
55.   True
56.   Max Dennison
57.   Salem
58.   Winifred, Sarah, Mary
59.   a cat
60.   Yes
61.   a virgin has to lit a candle
62.   Allison
63.   Dani
64.   Max lit a candle and brought back the Sanderson sisters
65.   No
66.   suck the life out of all children in Salem
67.   Yes
68.   dancing spell
69.   the kids opened the sisters's spellbook, wich send a signal of its location
70.   the child must drink a potion
71.   Max

72.	they were transformed into statues and turned to dust
73.	B
74.	D
75.	C
76.	A
77.	C
78.	B
79.	C
80.	D
81.	C
82.	A
83.	C
84.	C
85.	B
86.	C
87.	B
88.	B
89.	A
90.	C
91.	C
92.	B
93.	C
94.	B
95.	A
96.	A
97.	A
98.	C
99.	C
100.	C
101.	B
102.	C
103.	A

Made in the USA
Monee, IL
25 September 2022

14581247R00028